Ashley Sugarnotch

&

the WOLF

Elizabeth Deanna Morris Lakes

Mason Jar Press | Baltimore, MD

Additional Praise for
Ashley Sugarnotch & the Wolf

I love the feel of the language of this book, in my mouth, in my throat, in my eyes and hands and hair. I love Ashley Sugarnotch and her wolf, and if you read this book, you will too.

> —Amber Sparks,
> author of *I Do Not Forgive You*

These headlong, heartstrong poems tell pathos with a lyric ear, a chest full of windmills, a body peeled back, and a dark river rushing when everyone should be asleep but isn't.

> —Thea Brown
> author of *Famous Times*

This book is a model against forgetting, a spell against erasure, a disenchantment of the stories and dreams that make us feel safe.

> —Alina Stefanescu,
> author of *Every Mask I Tried On*

Ashley Sugarnotch & the Wolf is a bracing examination of trauma and the residue of guilt trauma leaves behind. Morris Lakes' debut will leave you undone.

> —Gabriel Blackwell
> author of *Madeleine E.*

These persona poems, deft in their ability to evoke both fear and the eerily familiar, reckon with the everyday violence of rape culture, like a myth we keep repeating, and ask why nothing ever changes.

> —Ruth Awad
> author of *Set to Music a Wildfire*

These poems draw blood.

—Catherine Pierce,
author of *The Tornado Is the World*

These heart-breaking, intelligent poems are also formally deft investigations into the power of beauty—beauty of language, of image, of story, and ultimately, surpassingly, of kindness.

—Jennifer Atkinson,
author of *The Thinking Eye*

Morris Lakes is the feminist poet we direly need today.

—Alyse Knorr,
author of *Mega-City Redux*

Disturbing and sublime, this book undoes what's been done and then does it anew, like sewing shut and licking reopen a fresh raw wound.

—Molly Gaudry,
author of *We Take Me Apart*

I devoured this book. This book devoured me.

—Hannah Gordon
managing editor of *Cheap Pop*

Elizabeth Deanna Morris Lakes has invented a new Little Red Riding Hood. Her name is Ashely Sugarnotch, like a sweet thing charred at the edges.

—Sabrina Orah Mark
author of *Wild Milk*

Published by
Mason Jar Press
Baltimore, MD 21218

Printed by Spencer Printing in Honesdale, PA.

Learn more about Mason Jar Press at masonjarpress.xyz.

Poems in this book originally appeared in *The Birds We Piled Loosely, Pioneertown Lit, Gulf Stream Literary Magazine,* and *Always Crashing.*

The poem, "Ashley Sugarnotch & the Big Red Bow" is partially an ekphrastic poem to Bob Diven's painting, "Red Bow."

The poem, "The Wolf: A Shadow Manifested" owes a gratitude to mewithoutYou's song, "Wolf am I! (And Shadow)."

for Kenny

Thank you for helping to make me iambic.

Poems

"If I do well I am blessed
 whether any bless me or not, and if I do
  ill I am cursed." We watch the moon rise
on the Susquehanna.

—Marianne Moore

The river is not just the river but holds legends in relief.

—Karla Kelsey

Thinking if it had a name it would have a solution / thinking if
I called a wolf a wolf I might dull its fangs.

—Kaveh Akbar

Ashley Sugarnotch
& the
WOLF

We All Think We Know About the Wolf

The huntsman doesn't always come.
Sometimes the Wolf eats up Little Red,
her grandmother already digesting.
Another time: Red complained

of her own hunger, and the Wolf
provided her grandmother's body
as an offering: teeth as hard as rice,
jaw as red as meat, blood as red as wine.

Red undressed and climbed into bed.
Devoured. In one, a cat whispers
that Red is a slut as she chews
on her parsed-out grandmother,

a little cannibal slut. The cat left
but that time, Red survived, clever
enough to realize the discrepancy
in the Wolf's face. And isn't it so easy

to disregard the beast? As easy
as it is for him to devour the girl.

Ashley Sugarnotch and the Big Red Bow

I just hate how thin and toned my legs are. My arm and leg hairs are so light I barely even have to shave. Can't my body be a little lopsided? One leg shorter than the other? I saw a young girl at the mall with these shoes, one wedge and the other flat. It compensated. I want to need to compensate. An old friend was born with two thumbs on one hand. Her parents cut one off—a shame for sure—but with the one she had left, L-shaped, she could smash anyone in thumb wrestling. She called it The Sledgehammer. My fingers? Even in winter, the cuticles don't tear. Even chewing them. Maybe I wouldn't mind looking so lovely and framed if I had something like heart surgery and a scar I could show off with strapless dresses. We weren't rich growing up; we were comfortable. If I had needed the surgery, or those shoes, we could have afforded it. This isn't so ridiculous, what I'm asking. My mother and father smoked cigars occasionally, had a glass of wine with friends. But these points of decay don't interest me. I'm not interested in some death film only visible when my body is pieced apart during autopsy. Even my ears are the same shape. Maybe something will just happen, you know? Some sort of accident or mishap. My father lost a chunk of ear during a war or something similar. He would always touch toward the blank space at the dinner table to remind us of something we couldn't know. But this was before. I am trying to know the things I can't. For Halloween, I wore my green swimsuit bottoms and a big red bow tied around my chest, a new car and a new car model. Everyone asked what I was. When I told them a present to be presented, they tugged at the bow end and looked past my eyes.

Ashley Sugarnotch and a World of

When I was a kid, when imagining what to wish when given wishes (every child is supposed to have wishes), I wondered if I should wish to feel all the pain in my life at once. Even then I knew it would kill me. I began to calculate how I could spread it out. Should I get it over once a year, like vaccines? Have I ever said that my mother was murdered? Shot by my father, for reasons I'm unsure of. After the shooting, I was basically an orphan. For all legal purposes, I was. Except when you're already 18, they don't use words like "orphan" anymore. I was in the house. My father turned himself in, and when the police arrived, they found my mother, and then me. In my room watching the light wind out from the fan blades. Center still but unfurling. The papers said, "unharmed." When I learned about the golden ratio, I saw my pain like a part of nature, a shell or a bean pole, spiraling from a center point. Out and out. When I feel myself spiraling now, I count. Lie as still as possible; count. I imagine that I am a circle, my mother is pi. And I believe that I have such perfect space, that each thing about me is even, calculable. Every time I start to tell a story, I stop believing it.

The Wolf Is the Wolf

i've become quite skilled at pretending to be
myself. at waking up at five-thirty barely
alive and fumbling toward the light

switch. i pull on khakis a button down
shirt. i drive still dozing something at which
i've become quite skilled: at pretending to be

awake. professional. steamed and pressed.
i always hope to catch you in the elevator
alive and fumbling toward the light.

to see your fingers press in the button
each tiny muscle contracting. is this what
i've become? quite skilled at pretending to be

aloof beside you scanning the ceiling my watch.
i'd like my fingers in your mouth your tongue
alive and fumbling toward the light.

when the door opens i trace the path to my desk.
i smile at the receptionist. check e-mail.
i've become quite skilled at pretending to be
alive and fumbling towards the light.

The Wolf and the Cup of Tea

this: the first time
that i saw you
ashley. in my
chair at my desk
i can see right
into the break
room. your first day
you came down for
coffee but the
carafe: empty.
instead you pulled
the hot water
spigot on the
coffee maker
and filled your mug
with the steamy
sputtering flow.
when you placed the
tea bag in you
let your finger
tips sink in too.
i counted to ten
before you drew them
out. the look on

your face: relief.
jaw slackened, cheeks
flushed. i knew i
loved you then loved
every last sweet
cranny. you knew
hate is defined
as spitting out
each other's mouths.
you knew pleasure
in sucking one's
raw fingers which
you did as you
left the moment
returned back to
the moments of
others. that night
i plunged my whole
hand into hot
tea and dreamt you
licked every last
finger.

Ashley Sugarnotch and her Mother

My mother's voice clicked softly like ivory coins in the thickness of night, hushing me as she would slowly pull the handle of my door and—hinges squeaking small like a whinny—sneak inside to sleep on the braided rag rug beside my bed. *Close your eyes, little one. Keep sleeping.* I did, because my mother said so. When I would wake next, the sunshine screaming through the window, my mother would be gone, already drinking coffee, face put on and dressed. Except once. I woke in the reticent dusk to see her curled on the rug facing the door, hands balled into fists. In the grayness, I decided to believe that the murk in bloom on her neck was the slightness of shadow, not yet illuminated by day.

The Wolf and the Wall

i must have been four/five.
i was with my mother
at the park running or
jumping. i ran to a
wall that cut against a
small hill. i ran from its
low base toward its peak.
flying. arms outstretched then
falling my clumsy foot
misplaced. my head on the
pavement clattering. i
should have blacked out instead
some white white burn enclosed
my skull. something so hot/
cold you can't at first tell
which. my mother ran quick
to me and as she grasped
for my body i clawed
for her face. she said my
name and i balled up the
act into my own fists.

Ashley Sugarnotch and the River

Some days, I swim across the river to an island covered with moss and lie out in the sun to burn. First, the sun sucks the water off my skin, before drawing it into redness and sweat. Then the flies come, the large peony ants, and crawl over my neck, routing their way from the line behind my ear to the muscles that blur the definition between neck and shoulder. It's my thighs where they bite. I don't move, I don't flick my feet, but instead find a circle of stillness. My sweat sinks into the moss and I am grateful for the respite of affection, these hair-thin fingers that crawl over my body. The wind is like a shadow along the current. Sometimes a boat passes. Do they see me on the shore? Once, a child flung a kite into the air, a small diamond of primary colors in the sky. I am waiting for my body to fill with air like the kite, for someone holding a string so my skin is taut, and I am distanced but unable to billow away. Full, finally, of some *thing*. Once I slept and when I woke my skin was chilled and bumpy with dried sweat. A storm had begun. I waded into the water, sky shouting overhead, and swam back to the shore. But halfway I paused. The river was a wide road, unreal with green and orange. Lightning chained across the neck of sky above the horizon. I stood and waited for the lightning to creep upstream, to fill this grave of a body like a flash bulb. When I finally got home, I stood under the hot water in the shower until it ran out. I buried myself under blankets as if it was winter.

The Wolf and the Distinct Feeling

do you have the distinct feeling
of atrophy ashley? not you
but the sense of thinning out our
world? i ran over a dead squirrel
today his uncrushed bones pinching
flat against the road. he never
had a chance. they're so quick too.
how was he ever crushed? power's
been out since eight. i never left

my bed. just watched the storms burst and swell rise/
fall. at ten i saw nothing until the
lightning dashed darkness into day. but then
the whole picture became exposed. where are
you tonight ashley? i watched last summer
you wade in the river and wait. sky
splitting open hoping if moss wouldn't
grow into your hair that lightning would melt
your legs together toes and fingers webbed.

(my hands could melt you
shut. they have such heat.)

i hardly knew you then
but you never did it
again never once were
willing to wait for some
thing to happen. there is
not enough world left for
you. it's atrophying
ashley. more than just moss
not growing. before rain
i heard only a lone
cicada. it landed

in my lap.
what aren't you
waiting for?

Ashley Sugarnotch Finds her Mother

What difference does it make whether I was in the house or not in the house—out at the store picking up some things: plastic bottles of various sizes, boxes made of thin cardboard, then checking out with a still-novel debit card, to then return to find—or whether I stayed home in my room, folding and putting away laundry, just about to leave for college, looking around like *why didn't I ever spruce this place up,* the room awash with pastel colors, dusty, like the memory of what color should have been, whether or not and either way the sound shattering through the house like a door slamming harder than doors can slam would shoot outward, and either I would walk downstairs and see her, or open up the front door, and see her, my mother, bent in the impossible shape death allows, blood splattered but not pooling, her eyes still shut in terror and my father: already gone.

The Wolf Always Dreams

ashley i
dreamt about you
again last night. we sat in my
room all golden brown light dust puffing up from piles

and piles
of books. sitting at
my feet legs bent to the side and
i read to you from books while you fingered

the hem of
my khakis touched the
round bone of my ankle. you moved
to your knees touched my lapels. i wasn't even in

a chair just
perched on a crate or
a stack of books. you twisted the
ends of my moustache and then pulled like velcro

gave yourself
a unibrow. you stuck your
hands into the armholes of my
sweater-vest squeezed the blades. but i couldn't get any

closer. i was
static as statue.
i miss the days in our dreams when
we would lie with our heads on the curb legs in the street

and wait for
the bus. the bus would
never come though. it was cloudy
and we didn't worry about our legs getting run

over or
our faces sun
burnt. sometimes i think we're meeting
in these dreams. midnight tryst. when i see you next after

the night you
blush you know you've spent
the night asleep in me touching
the edges of me. while i remember how you let me reach
my hand forward and press my palm around your cheek. the

line of your jaw like a corner.

Ashley Sugarnotch Is Curious

I'm curious about forgiveness. I read an 85-year-old nun forgave her 19-year-old rapist. She did so "by God's merciful grace." Okay, yes, I cried all over when I read about her forgiveness, but I'm still not sure what it means. Who wins? Because let's not pretend this evens and absolves. Even she admitted that she now knows terror; her sleep is restless. And yet she said, "Of course; he is forgiven." I wonder if the boy will lie in his cell at night, the sound outside the bars never ceasing like a chorus of yelling crickets, the lights never turned off, enduring dusk, and think to himself that he was bathed clean by her words. Was her gesture simply habit? Did the language she had spoken so many times before come out by muscle memory? And why is this what we want to hear? What a neat little package: he's now in jail, she's forgiven him, justice has been served. I am sure that woman felt rage and asked her god for forgiveness for feeling it. Perhaps those prayers did soothe her. Because: where can rage lead if not sloughed off?

Ashley Sugarnotch Grows a Tomato

My tomato sprouted; rather, the tomato I threw into the back yard this spring is growing a thin stem. I bought the tomato so that I could put slices on sandwiches. But when I cut it open, the inside was already black, rotten. I'm really not much of a gardener. But I love my new yellow stem. It's slender and bends to one side like it's reaching. At first, I was concerned about its yellow color, its lack of chlorophyll. I tenderly watered it, made sure to place mulch and fertilize it, to stake it with a skewer (the plant is that small.) But it still didn't grow. Yet it didn't just die. I could have tried to transplant it, moved it to another part of the yard, but I won't. A philosopher once wrote that it is a human's right to suffer, so I bestow that right to my tomato plant. If it wants to bend over and let its top touch the ground, it can, and I won't bother it anymore.

The Wolf Wonders if Ashley's Ripe

i stewed blackberries for
dessert last night ashley and discovered

something marvelous. the
berries dark as ever when raw turn bright

red when exposed to heat.
then as you stir they burst. each pustule,

each heart surrounding a
seed disintegrated to a tart slime.

but i think they're supposed
to be like that. pre-grown full blisters. i

tear my blisters open
always. the liquid inside is blood with

-out the blood parts—the red/
white blood cells platelets. serum. not even

the coagulants are
left. i only knew this because i looked

it up. how could i now
recognize blood without everything that

made it so? blisters are
supposed to protect us just like the juice

sacs surrounding the black-
berry seeds. but the blisters just hurt. they

are swelling from attacks
our skin couldn't handle. the berries when

cooled lost their jeweled red sheen.
i need to stop comparing you to fruit

ashley. i'm not good at
this at being a human like the rest

of us. but you are. you
see fruit for fruit, even if you can't see

your own form as right your
body and mind as one composed piece. i'm

sure you saw the blisters
on your feet too and wondered what let your

body change without asking you first.

Ashley Sugarnotch and the Earthquake

We had an earthquake today. Of course, I was nowhere near the epicenter, but I felt it, the shaking cubicles, my boss jumping up like she had heard a gunshot or bomb. But it wasn't so explosive. The feeling just crawled up the east coast, tickling the bones in our ears. In the cubicle next to me, the woman said she just felt this unease creep on her, a ghost. The decadence of the earthquake making everyone else suddenly aware of their bodies in relation to their desks, the ground. In California, their quakes don't creep like ours do. There are too many breaks in the crust—the tremors can't bridge the gaps. We were luckier, single plates letting landslides occur four times as far. We were caught gasping, the waves of earth's fingers creeping into our spines.

Ashley Sugarnotch Is Not Interested in Love

I am not interested in love. Today I saw a wolf that had been hit by a car. But it looked like it had been *eaten* by a car. The blood looked like a giant bow on a brand-new vehicle, except it was tying closed the road. See, that's way more interesting than hearing an anecdote about how I tenderly, under many blankets held hands last night with someone I had very much wanted to hold hands with for a very long time. (Which, in actuality, I did not). Instead, last night, I watched a documentary on giant squid. Giant squid have teeth-rimmed suckers, hundreds of tiny crowns. (I thought about holding hands with the squid, under the water, no scuba suit required. The water around our hands blossoming into roses.) I am not interested in pursuit. In "making memories." I saw a movie once where two people licked each other's faces and then cut off slivers of the other's legs. In the end, they turned into whales. It was supposed to be a movie representing marriage. But those two people from the movie got divorced. And now that I know that, I want to watch it backwards to undo it. That's what I want: my body undone, untransformed.

The Wolf, The Bird, and the Burrs

while waiting
for you today ashley by the river i
saw a

movement in the
brush along the shore. as i moved closer i
noticed

flapping. a bird
was caught in burrs. its feathers so close to the
plant's stem.

did you know that
burrs inspired velcro? but velcro is tamed
compared

to hooks that bite
into skin and fur. that rip away when pulled.
the bird

battled. had it
simply landed? tried to rest? i couldn't bear
its struggle.

i tried to un-
hook its wings from the trap to give another
chance to

fly. the bird pecked
at my hands. i bled. once freed the bird couldn't
move well.

it foundered in
the dust. had it always been broken or had
i snapped

some essential
hollow bone? the bird cried from the ground. i pressed
my foot

on its head. cracked.
this wasn't what i intended ashley. i
wanted

to set it free.
instead i ended its suffering. a gift
or what?

The Wolf Asks

if i
ask forgiveness
now will it rinse me of
the guilt heavy like ballast stones
sinking?

Ashley Sugarnotch Was the Hunter

When I find myself mired in the shock and sizzle of loss or violence, I inevitably resort to examining my body and wondering how to mark it. Mildly, I'll trim my nails, file them, intricately paint them. Bring a cup of sugar into the shower and exfoliate. Shave all points of my body. Then always to my hair, holding the scissors up to it, fingering the fake loops of hair by the dyes, considering the chestnut brown, the "red" that's really wine or maroon. Reconsidering bangs. Then it's the idea of fasting, of yoga, stillness and settling. If my skeleton is really jumping out of my skin, I must overcome the urge to mark my body with ink. Marking it would make it mine, I think. But I never do. I go to the river and burn in the sun, let my body sink into the mud by the bank. Because isn't that all I am anyway: dirt and water recomposed into movement and thought?

Ashley Sugarnotch Will
Not Leave the Wolf Alone

oh dear it's begun again. when i
see you in the break room with your hot coffee

scanning the newspaper looking for
a sign i'm staring at the way you lean more

on one leg than the other. of course
i had a dream about you last night. this used

to happen once in a while. now
it happens once a week. "what i would like you

to recognize," you told me. we were
leaning against the bricks of some building. a

place where the grass reaches bottom
of the wall and teenagers sneak to make out.

"is what i leave for you." zipping down
the center of your sweatshirt, cracking to the

little windmills inside your chest, moist
linen taut around the frames of blades. i knew

you wanted me to reach inside. for
what? the heart was gone. the other organs too.

Ashley Doesn't Know

See, the thing is, I'm not even sure my goal here. Here, meaning on Earth. My boss asked me what my five-year plan was. I said *stay alive,* and she laughed. I wasn't kidding. I'm an only child—an orphan, really, because my parents are basically dead. No one's ever invited me to Thanksgiving. I don't have or want a cat. My favorite thing is the sun. Sometimes, I'll look through pictures of my family when I was younger. But it's all useless. What happens before doesn't matter now that I know the end. The twist is that my mom is dead, and I'm alone in an office with no windows, and at night I have nightmares that I feel certain will someday come true. How about we play two truths and a lie: I cradled her limp hand against my face. As he left the courtroom I spit in his face, but I missed. I sold the house.

The Wolf Attempts to Explain Himself

i just want this all to stop now to go away ashley.
the feeling that saturates my skin at night
like my skeleton is pulling away from my flesh. just
like it's new and implanted but rejecting my body.
an infection. i want to be whole and composed to last
through the night without shoving my hand in the hot water

or numbing my face with ice. the water
running down my neck. how do i stop this ashley?
my hands are full of static i can't squeeze out. the last
thing i want is to find you in my dreams tonight
and crack open your ribs and rid your body
of its organs. is it so unreasonable to want a justice

for myself? a new ending where i justify
i'm not a wolf inevitable. finding you in the water
of the river and holding you down your body
putting up a fight because that's human ashley.
it's human to fight against what we want at night
when the exhaustion wears through the last

set of reserve and control. i wonder when my last
guard will shatter and i'll become just
less than human. the other. unrecognizable at night

and willing to be held in straits beneath the water
until i can no longer breathe. it's so easy ashley
for them to see you as less than a body

and certainly not a soul. they won't see my body
full of electricity and my hands in fists trying to last
against the jerking muscles and teeth bitten on my tongue. ashley
you know i never want to hurt you in the dreams i just
lose myself when covered in fur. i'd rather bathe you in water
cool and blessed. i'd rather find you like a lover in the night

and curl at your feet. a good dog. and in this tender night
we'd know though our dreams might be bad our bodies
would be still. i'd wash you clean with river water
in the morning and our restfulness would last
through the day. but if i get too close i might just
forget these hands are mine ashley.

ashley, will either of us make it through the night just long enough
to see sun's body rise one last time over the river's sparkling water?

Ashley Sugarnotch Feels Awful

It's inappropriate to take naps at my desk. That's what my boss told me. I've been having trouble sleeping. I've searched the hell out of what to do. I cover all electric lights. I breathe in eight-counts. I soak lavender buds in hot water and sip the resulting tea as I read a light article on gardening or cooking—nothing apt to turn the knob on my adrenaline or heartbeat. Still, I lie and wait. Even through the pulled curtains, lights from pacing cars race by like fingers pushing across the ceiling. At three, when the cars calm down and even the crickets and cicadas begin to hush, I go outside. I walk, I walk in the grass, along the sidewalk, along the road. I walk until the stars begin to blur as my eyes water, until my legs tingle with their understanding of gravity. By now, it's five o'clock in the morning. My body will know nothing but rest. I make my way inside and fall onto the floor. I sleep. And immediately I dream of the rotting forest, the bald dirt hills, the pile of bricks where a house used to be. I don't even bother to run anymore. I sink, maybe hoping to fall asleep here, too, to wake up in some slightly calmer, slightly less decayed dreamscape. But I don't. The wolf comes, sometimes more dirt than fur. With delicate teeth, he bites my shoulder and pulls back the skin. The pain feels like electricity, both hot and cold and muscles jerking alive and wholly thickly dead. And so the wolf undresses me, one layer at a time, until I gasp and find myself with no lungs. And when I try again, my lungs fill; I am in the living room, crumpled on the carpet, itchy with sweat. What is one to do when left with pain like that? At the café near me, they have a drink called the Shakey. It's not on the menu anymore, but I started ordering it. Six shots of espresso, topped off with dark roasted coffee. My muscles vibrate after these, alive and shuddering in some way that is separate from myself. But then, they move, then they find their way to my desk, my work, the emails and meetings. But the wolf, I feel him waiting beneath the surface, waiting to strip me into pieces and call me *his*.

The Wolf Was the Runner

i fall asleep
sometimes and an
orchestra fills
my ears as if
i were in the
middle of the
pit. symphony
surging into
my ear canals.
when i awake
the sound is left
as memory
only. doesn't
your skull want to
jump out of your
head ashley? i
have been slamming
my head against
the door jamb at
night to sleep. it
helps. my hair can
cover up the
bruises. i found
you in the woods

last night ashley.
you had let the
tree's roots grow in-
to your organs
a vine crowned your
head. "now you can
understand this"
you told me. you
creaked open your
chest and the wind
mills were gone. now
metal larvae
crawled over your
redwhite bones. i
wrestled out your
heart. it flaked to
bits in my fingers.

Ashley Sugarnotch Was the Runner

When I fall asleep, sometimes an orchestra fills my ears. A symphony. As if I were suddenly submerged in sound. As soon as I become aware of it—as soon as I think—it wakes me back up. I'm left with the sound as a thought. I'm left with the feeling that something important just slipped between my fingers. When I finally slept last night, I found myself in the woods again. This time, I couldn't move. The roots of a tree had snarled around my wrists. The wolf came (as he always does) and peeled back the skin on my chest. Beneath, instead of muscle, were worms of molten metal crawling around and over each other, swarming my heart. All rust. The wolf snapped out the heart in his jaws and swallowed. I woke up as I said in to the air, "finally."

The Wolf: A Shadow Manifested

i died on a ship
last night in my dream.

the ship had sunk i
was in the only unsunk room

suppose then i didn't
actually die last night.

i had knowledge
of the end. aren't i already

dead? eventually
i'll slip. feel your life draining

over my hands. i
am waiting in the shadows

or rather i am
shadow waiting to transform

to action or mass.
do i fail

at being human?
or by fighting myself am

i more a human
afterall? i know this sounds

so rational ashley.
i can be rational when

you aren't near.
if i die who wins? i know

you do not want this
ashley but that doesn't mean

someone else wouldn't
find you. i'm not just any shadow.

i'm yours. i'm beside
you in darkness but even

more so in the light.

Ashley Sugarnotch Knows Your Number at 2 in the Morning

I wonder what it feels like to be a daughter to a father. I want to say it feels like being a daughter to a mother, but I'm not sure. I know being a daughter with no father feels like the walks I take at night in winter. I want to believe that the silence cuts deeper than the cold. Having a mother felt like having a second self, a second set of answers to my questions. This is supposed to be the same but it's not. It's not. These losses have left, not vacancies, but this: the rocks in the riverbed are sharp against my feet; the road is wider and harder to cross, like you just can't walk across fast enough; sun glare leaves phosphenes longer in my eyes, not blinded, but obstructed. Being a daughter to a mother turns my blood to stone. Being a daughter to a father whitewashes me in adrenaline. I will walk for hours.

The Wolf Knows Your
Number at 2 in the Morning

just cleaning up my phone

just cleaning up my phone
tomorrow who
is the crazy one now hey
ash i'm drinking
tonight

just cleaning up my phone
tomorrow who
is the crazy one now hey
ashley your wolf needs you i need
you to

just cleaning up my phone
tomorrow who
is the crazy one now hey
ashley

just cleaning up my phone

i miss you ashley your wolf
needs you right now i
need you please HELP me

hey

hey ashley

hey

just cleaning up my phone please
help me save myself

i love you

good night

good night

good night

good night i need to sleep now

love your

love you

Ashley Sugarnotch Just Wants You to Know

my father never called me from prison of course I never visited
him but he also never called and I hoped just once that he would
call so that I could see the number light up in my hand and I
could choose to not pick up the phone

The Wolf and the Little Bit of Water

i
cannot remember your body

ashley sugarnotch. i have
tried these nights tried to sketch you into
the sheets of graph paper that i used
to use to measure them out:
your slim
proportions.
the small of

your
back an arc in a two by three

rectangle. i started when
i was bored in our weekly meetings
and you, with your posture so straight, a
mannequin. this was before
i knew
you ashley
really knew

you.
before you visited me each

night. before you dipped your legs
into the river during the storm
hoping the lightning would zip closed your
spine. before you began to
drink hot
espresso
mid-day and

at
night to mix the steeped lavender

buds left over from your tea-
ball with honey. so you could eat them,
and maybe finally calm the fuck
down. but, i can remember
the blood.
how it was
wide, the ri-

ver,
your river, a current from your

neck down to your pelvis. you
said, "it feels like electricity."
you said, "i knew it."

CODA

Be Kind, Be Kind, Be Kind

after Dorothea Lasky

It feels like everyone is dead or about to leave me
Occasionally I watch YouTube interviews with Mr. Rogers
These make me cry a lot
Enough to have the tears tie together like bonnet strings
      beneath my chin
I could betray Mr. Rogers and he would still love me
I'm trying to write a poem about how Mr. Rogers makes me
      feel like there's a god
Well, not exactly
Makes me feel like those who believe must feel when they believe
I'm writing this poem after Dorothea Lasky, because I'm
      stealing her style
In her poems, she can say, "I am sad"
Without someone saying "That's a bad poem"
Or worse, "That's not a poem"
I can think of 12 people off the top of my head who've told me
      that they've been raped
Not from TV or books; people I knew personally
Some raped by more than one person, more than one time
I can't tell if the details matter or if they'd just make this poem
      seem more dramatic
Like: some of the rapists were teachers
Or: one was beaten and left her small town to get stitches and

for anonymity
Or: I'm still friends with one of the rapists
This is only a small part of atrocity
Mr. Rogers must have known about suffering
But he believed in listening and caring for everyone
Because everyone is human first and thus worthwhile
He would love this poem, because I'm trying to figure
        something out
He would ask me questions, thoughtfully, with quietness akin
        to care
He once said that there were three ways to ultimate success
"Be kind, be kind, be kind"
I will try, Mr. Rogers
I will try I will try I will try

Susquehanna

My river rolls low and slowly crawling
through the big heavy heart of Pennsylvania,
flattened a mile wide, washing its veins and
tributaries, which the Susquehanna receives,
and I am so grateful. The catfish hover
in shallows, shirking the current that pulls
at their tails. In a small swirling pool, I
sink in my feet, the water like cool hands
grasping my ankles. I would like to sink
so that only my face, exposed, looks like
nothing more than a glint on the water.

The Certainty of the Body

Twenty months after she disappeared, last seen
in Harrisburg. The boats search Memorial Lake for her body.

She was believed murdered. Pings of sonar
echo back to boats revealing logs, fish parts,

leaves, but mostly: muck. Murk of the cold
lake in late winter, nearly spring. Murk of each

organic object chilled and slowed in their rot.
The body, an insider claims, would be rolled

in a carpet. Each scanned log could be the body, disguised.
Critics will say: the 5- to 6-hour search is too short, shallow.

That the muted water obscures too harshly.
But the search continues to provide shallow comfort

for the father who stands by the lake in his jean
jacket and worn-in work shirt. They tell him

they won't be dragging the lake. They will not
send in divers to comb their fingers over every

log, seeing with their fingers fabric instead of bark, for bones
to push back from beneath the fabric. For the body,

moldering, to be unrolled and birthed. But the father
is not looking for a body in the lake, for the surety

of an end, the finite, the answer. The father still
searches for Kortne, the daughter who became

more than body when he named her.

Trisha

If the snow comes early, before all the leaves
have been stripped, the trees' branches will

be pulled low. Weak ones will snap. The still
moist scars will weep sap. The branches, ones

that could have produced more leaves, apples, acorns,
had the early snow not pulled them down,

lay prostrate in the street. Cars will slowly drive
around them. Some will tangle in wires, ripping

them from transistors. A quiet violence will beget
another quiet violence: a power outage. We will

sit quietly in the dark—and yes, it will be dark,
even in mid-Autumn, the brilliancy of summer still

sharp—waiting until we can sleep and then hoping
to dream, hoping that when the sun rises the roads

will be clear and the electricity will be surging
into our bulbs. When Trisha was murdered,

it was mid-January. The trees stripped bare.
It snowed just a bit, little stings of ice.

I can't help but wonder if Trisha wore a coat,
a sweater. Was she warm? Did the layers absorb

the blood as it left her? She was shot in the stomach,
eighteen weeks pregnant for the second time.

Another's child. She was found in her ex-boyfriend's
bed, her ex-boyfriend alive beside her. Shouldn't this be

a metaphor, like the trees and the branches?
In prison for twenty to forty years, what will he

see when he walks out into the day? What will the wind
feel like against his face?

Statement

After she was blackout drunk, Richard walked Anya home
to the house he shared with his wife, who made a bed
on their couch, tucked Anya in, and kissed her forehead.
They had been out bar-hopping, starting at the craft brewery
and ending at the dive, all in a tenth of a mile on Market Street.
Anya was 21. Richard was over 40.

I didn't find out until later that on this walk "home,"
in the dive bar's alley (the alley shared with the restaurant
where I worked, where I might have been), Richard
bent the blackout drunk Anya over and raped her.
It was not the first time he raped her. Anya said
when his wife kissed her forehead, she felt loved.

≈≈≈

The house Richard and his wife rented was by the Susquehanna.
Dog sitting for Richard, I also napped on the couch
Anya slept on that night. I drank jasmine tea
that reminded me of spring. I walked the dog
along the river, and the postman, seeing the brown
mutt he knew so well, left a treat on the road
for us to discover when we traversed up the block.
What could go wrong in a world like that?

≈≈≈

Richard cornered Anya and me once in the café where Anya
worked. He said, "Why don't we just go for a ride? Come on,
let's just go, let's just go for a ride and talk." Anya refused.
He pressed again and I said, "She said no, Richard." He looked
at me and snarled, "You know nothing." Anya looked up—
her head had been buried in her hands—
and said, "She knows everything."
Richard moved out of our way, and we ran to Anya's car.
Got home. Locked the front door. Checked every window.
Pulled every shade.

≈≈≈

On afternoons, I would ride my bike across
the green metal bridge over Penn's Creek
and ride along the water, the breeze
warm and billowy, an embrace. Once, Anya
and I drove along it at night, smoking cigarettes
(I, inhaling like a cigar), and stared out.
With no lights on the other shore, the river was flat black,
stone. We couldn't hear it lap and ebb. It absorbed
any nearby light. We turned around and drove back.

≋

I wish I could untwine Anya's experiences with violence
from her desertion of me. In the end, after Anya broke
it off with Richard, after he stalked us, after I held
her in my bed at night and fell a little bit in love,
she disappeared. Stopped calling, stopped answering,
stopped.

Between me and Anya, I can only see me. I see:
I slept in your bed at night. I protected you.
It was your turn to take care of me. I. I. I.

≋

Richard could have killed us. I'm not saying this
to be dramatic. I'm saying it because he was huge,
because he raped Anya, because what would
have happened if she had gotten in the car. If
I had, in a misguided attempt at protection,
gone with them?

≋

The last time I saw Anya, she was a mile or two
away. I had just had knee surgery and couldn't walk,
couldn't drive. Finally, I was the one certifiably injured.
She wanted to meet me somewhere before she
flew home to the west coast. When I said I couldn't,
she said, "Oh, maybe next time then." As if our paths
could cross so easily.

Anya has an I tattooed on her spine, at the top
of her neck. "You would," I thought.

"If you kill Ashley at the end," another poet tells me
"then you're supporting violence against women."
We're at a sports bar and have to yell over
the sound of other patrons whooping at the TVs
that surround us. I am appalled. He looks at me
like I literally have her blood on my hands.

I'm much more interested in care
than in love. I can care for someone
I've just met. Anya first appeared
in my life as she left. She called—
we had swapped numbers when
grouped together for a class project.
She was crying. She was
on the street outside my house.
I let her in, wrapped her
in a blanket, brewed tea, listened.
She didn't have much to say, only:
"It's about my dad." After I
learned about the affair, I asked,
"That night was about Richard
wasn't it?" And she nodded.

I would never take back that night
when she appeared and I took her
into my arms, though I realize if I had not
picked up, that I wouldn't have
been there for the aftermath of the affair.
How could I leave her in the dark
of my street, hoping I'd pick up
and let her in?

My professor asks me why I'm writing
these poems, these poems that try to
reenact non-verbal trauma through language.
I mumble and grapple my way
through explaining that these poems
take place along the Susquehanna
River. Later, I wish I had said,
"I write these poems because I care
  about my heart which is somewhere
  in that river."

I lived along the river for the first 23 years
of my life, either in Harrisburg or at the university
that bears the river's name. I was born
in a hospital that overlooked the city's
seven bridges. This river runs
like a wide brush through my life.
Frames my life. This river buoyed me,
a constant.

My professor's name is also Richard.
The first few times we emailed,
I cringed away from the screen when
I saw his name, afraid the old Richard
had found me. Even though the rapes,
the affair, the violence weren't
mine.

≈≈≈

I don't know how to end this poem.
I don't know how because this poem
is trying to talk about things I can't
put to an end. Ashley always dies—
my hands didn't hold the knife.

As I write this last stanza, I'm sitting
in a café on State Street, the river
to my left and the green-domed
capital to my right. I don't live
in Pennsylvania anymore. Can I write
this, these violences, if I can't
even claim this place? I want to believe
the river's ingrained in my body. I want to

believe these poems, my trying, can
mean something to someone other
than myself.

Elizabeth Deanna Morris Lakes was born in Harrisburg, PA and has a BA in Creative Writing from Susquehanna University and an MFA from George Mason University. She has appeared in *Always Crashing, The Rumpus, Cartridge Lit, Crab Fat Magazine, SmokeLong Quarterly,* and *cahoodaloodaling.* She has a chapbook, *Patterning,* from Corgi Snorkel Press. She is co-host of The Smug Buds, a podcast.

Acknowledgements

First and foremost, to my four favorite people in the order I met them: Margaret Morris (Mom!), Blake Morris (brother!), Kenny Lakes (lovelight!), & Elliott Lakes (child!). Also Rudy, our very orange cat.

To my motherpoets: Jen Atkinson and Karla Kelsey. To my teachers: Gary Fincke (my writing grandfather), Catherine Dent, Sally Keith, Eric Pankey, and my dear adviser, Peter Streckfus-Green.

To the writers that stand like lighthouses in my life: Sarah Gzemski (Little Gzem, "I talk to you every day, & I miss you every day."), William Hoffacker (my pod-wife), Dana Diehl (sunlight), Kim Stoll (Kimby Cakes), Michael V. Coakley (who is somehow nicknameless) and, of course, Joseph Scapellato (my dream guardian). For Amber Cook, Melissa Goodrich, Theresa Beckhusen, & Lauren Bailey—Perf 10! For my grad school cohort, especially Ah-reum Han, Alyssa Dandrea, Alicia Padovich, and Ryan Meyer. For the writers who have always been there for me, in ways I probably didn't deserve: James Dunham, Kathryn Watson, Alyse Knorr, Kate Partridge, Jay Patel, Jessica McCaughey, and Sal Pane. To the writers I'm so glad to know from the internet and occasionally in real life: Berry Grass, Tasha Coryell, Brian Oliu,

Matt Bell, Sam Martone, and Amber Sparks—Thank you for helping me feel connected to the writing community.

For Adrian Zylawy, my penpal and the first poet I truly loved, and Nathan J. Robinson, my favorite band.

Thanks to Mason Jar Press for seeing my book and thus seeing me, especially Michael Tager, Ashley Miller, and Ian Anderson.

For Pennsylvania: *Keystone State, Motherfucker.*

And thanks to every reader that read the acknowledgements first. (I do it too!)

Other Mason Jar Press Titles

...and Other Disasters
short stories by Malka Older

Manhunt
a novella by Jaime Fountaine

The Couples
a novella by Nicole Callihan

All Friends Are Necessary
a novella by Tomas Moniz

Continental Breakfast
poetry by Danny Caine

How to Sit
memoir by Tyrese Coleman

Broken Metropolis
an anthology of queer speculative fiction
edited by Dave Ring

I am Not Famous Anymore
poems by Erin Dorney

Learn more at masonjarpress.xyz